INTRODUCTION

Systems of Life celebrates its 20th anniversary this year. When the series first appeared in *Nursing Times,* professional education was very different and those early series were probably useful adjuncts to the conventionally taught anatomy and physiology course or handy revision notes for the student nurse facing examinations.

It is a mark of Systems of Life's quality that it has re-invented itself and survived a revolution in nursing education. Nowadays we understand that it is often used by qualified nurses who are increasingly conscious of the need to revise and update their knowledge, and by students who find that it complements the new style of learning in which they are encouraged to seek out information themselves from a variety of sources.

Congratulations to the Systems of Life team – writer, Dr Anne Roberts, illustrator, Peter Gardiner and desk editor, Jean Cullinan – on another classic work.

Blood

Blood consists of red cells, white cells and platelets, suspended in plasma.
People have between 3.5 and 5 litres of blood, depending on their size and gender;
in general, women have a smaller blood volume than men.

Functions of blood
1. Transport
2. Buffering acid-base balance
3. Defence of body against infection and other threats.

Blood as a transport system

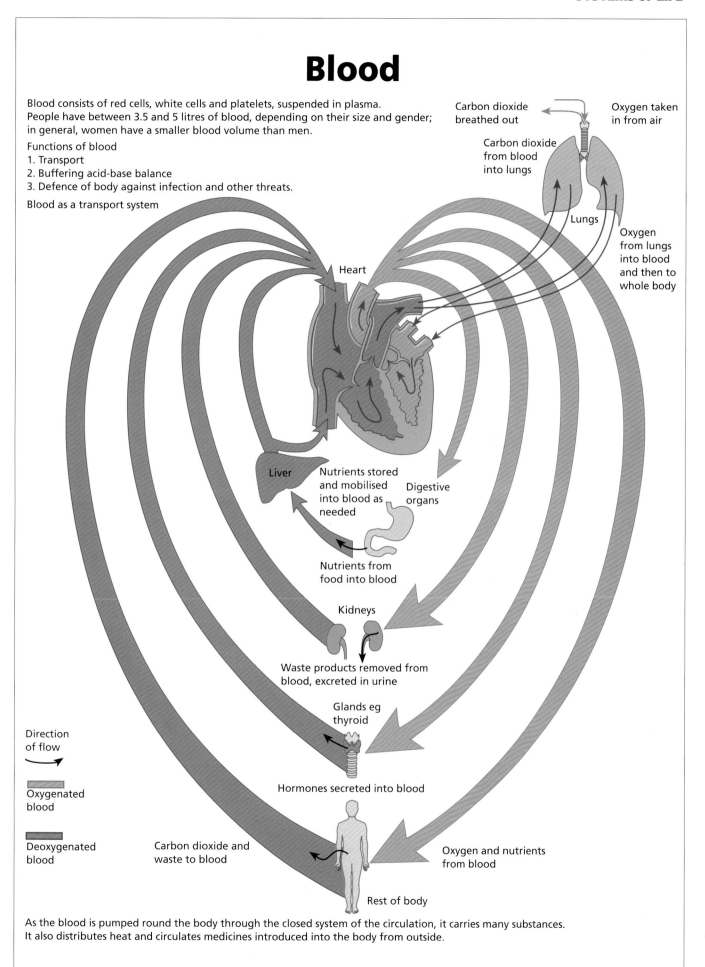

Carbon dioxide breathed out

Oxygen taken in from air

Carbon dioxide from blood into lungs

Lungs

Oxygen from lungs into blood and then to whole body

Heart

Liver

Nutrients stored and mobilised into blood as needed

Digestive organs

Nutrients from food into blood

Kidneys

Waste products removed from blood, excreted in urine

Glands eg thyroid

Hormones secreted into blood

Direction of flow

Oxygenated blood

Deoxygenated blood

Carbon dioxide and waste to blood

Oxygen and nutrients from blood

Rest of body

As the blood is pumped round the body through the closed system of the circulation, it carries many substances.
It also distributes heat and circulates medicines introduced into the body from outside.

Red blood cells (RBCs), or erythrocytes

In healthy adults, red blood cells are produced in the bone marrow.
In the fetus they are also made in the liver and spleen, and this happens in adults with some blood diseases.

They are shaped like discs, concave on both sides, consisting of a membrane envelope containing the red pigment haemoglobin.
This substance picks up oxygen in the lungs, carries it round the body as oxyhaemoglobin and releases it in the hypoxic tissues.
Each RBC is 7.5μ (microns) across and 2μ thick.
They have to squeeze through the smaller capillaries, but this gets the haemoglobin closer to the tissues for gas exchange purposes.

Production of red cells is stimulated by the hormone erythropoietin.
This is mainly produced by the kidney, but a small amount comes from the liver.
When the tissues are short of oxygen (hypoxia), erythropoietin secretion is increased
 and red cell production is stepped up.
The new RBCs can carry extra oxygen, so the hypoxia is corrected.
Once this has happened, erythropoietin secretion and RBC production both return to normal.

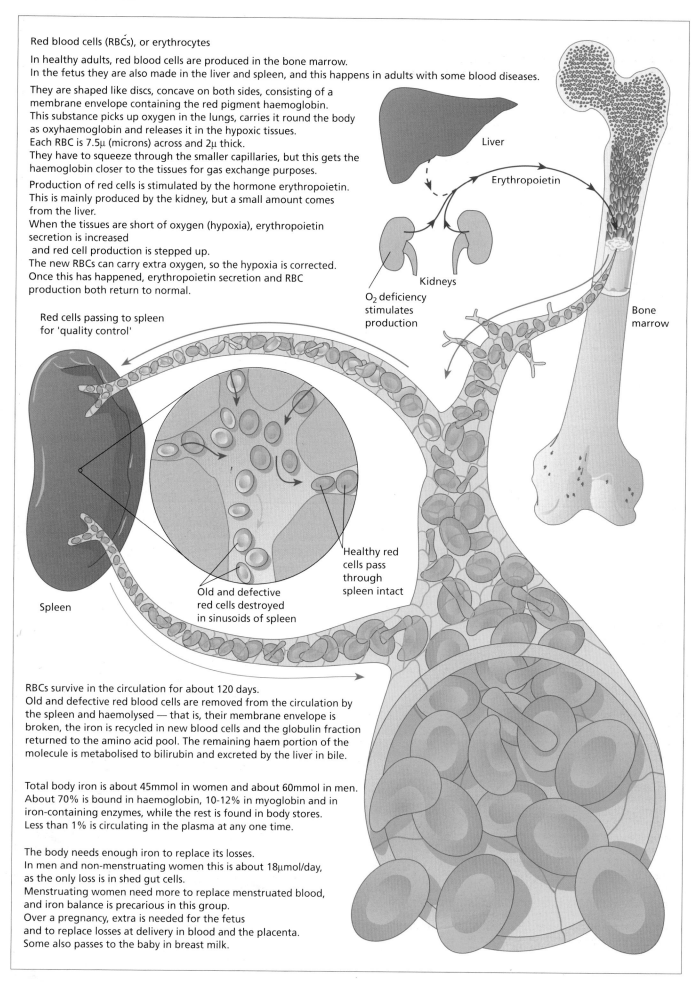

Liver

Erythropoietin

Kidneys

O$_2$ deficiency
stimulates
production

Bone
marrow

Red cells passing to spleen
for 'quality control'

Healthy red
cells pass
through
spleen intact

Old and defective
red cells destroyed
in sinusoids of spleen

Spleen

RBCs survive in the circulation for about 120 days.
Old and defective red blood cells are removed from the circulation by the spleen and haemolysed — that is, their membrane envelope is broken, the iron is recycled in new blood cells and the globulin fraction returned to the amino acid pool. The remaining haem portion of the molecule is metabolised to bilirubin and excreted by the liver in bile.

Total body iron is about 45mmol in women and about 60mmol in men.
About 70% is bound in haemoglobin, 10-12% in myoglobin and in iron-containing enzymes, while the rest is found in body stores.
Less than 1% is circulating in the plasma at any one time.

The body needs enough iron to replace its losses.
In men and non-menstruating women this is about 18μmol/day, as the only loss is in shed gut cells.
Menstruating women need more to replace menstruated blood, and iron balance is precarious in this group.
Over a pregnancy, extra is needed for the fetus
and to replace losses at delivery in blood and the placenta.
Some also passes to the baby in breast milk.

Iron metabolism

People at particular risk of iron deficiency are:
Older infants, children and adolescents who are growing rapidly,
especially if intake is poor.
Pregnant women.
Women with heavy periods.
Anyone losing blood — eg from piles or elsewhere in the gut.
People who have had gastric surgery and lack hydrochloric acid.

Iron from food is most easily taken into the body as haem in blood; liver,
meat and also fish are good sources.
A vegetarian diet contains less iron, but extra vitamin C from fruit and
vegetables helps absorption.

Phytates in flour, and some medicines (eg antacids, tetracycline)
inhibit iron absorption.

Small intestine

Iron is absorbed in the upper small
intestine; it can only cross cell walls
in the ferrous form (Fe^{++})

Stomach

Ferric (Fe^{+++}) iron is
reduced to ferrous (Fe^{++})
form by gastric acid or by
vitamin C from diet.

Intestinal cell

Ferritin
(Fe^{+++})

Fe^{++}

Alkaline intestinal juice
inhibits iron absorption

Leaves cell
as Fe^{++}

Combines with protein to
form transferrin in blood Fe^{+++}

Stored as haemosiderin
(Fe^{+++})and ferritin
(Fe^{+++}) in liver, spleen
and bone marrow

Incorporated into new
haemoglobin during
red cell manufacture;
(Fe^{++} ; Fe^{+++}
will not carry oxygen).

When old red cells are destroyed, iron is
returned to bone marrow stores for re-use.

The absorbed iron is taken into the blood and combined
with a transport protein to form transferrin.
Some of this goes direct to the bone marrow for immediate
use in the haemoglobin of new red cells.
The rest is stored as haemosiderin and ferritin in the liver,
spleen and bone marrow.

Faeces

Remainder stays in
mucosal cells and is
eventually shed with
them in stools

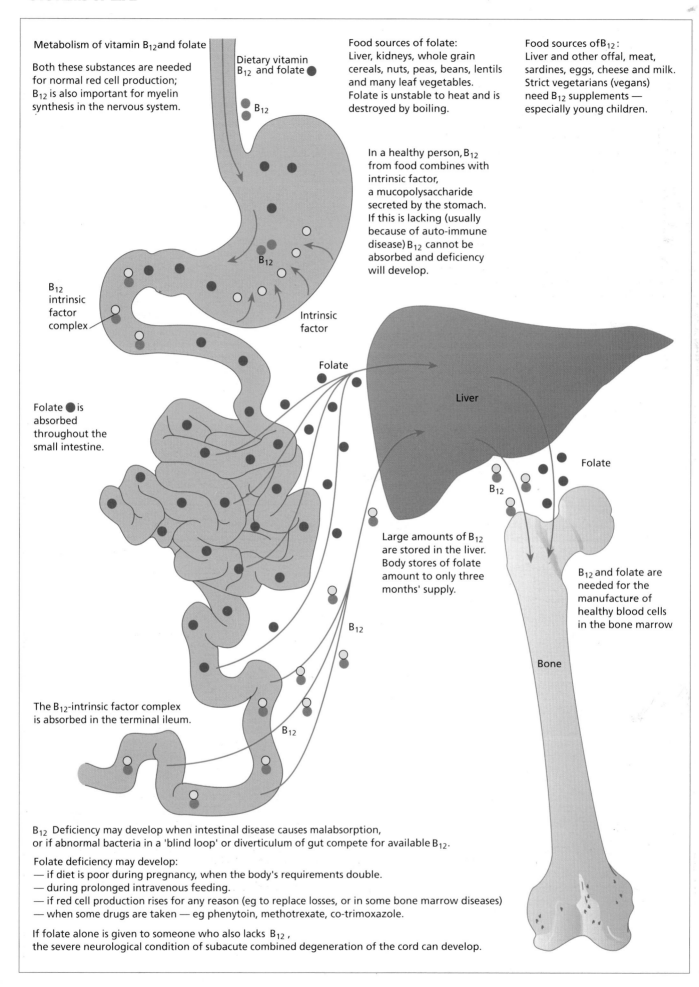

Metabolism of vitamin B_{12} and folate

Both these substances are needed for normal red cell production; B_{12} is also important for myelin synthesis in the nervous system.

Dietary vitamin B_{12} and folate ●

B_{12}

Food sources of folate: Liver, kidneys, whole grain cereals, nuts, peas, beans, lentils and many leaf vegetables. Folate is unstable to heat and is destroyed by boiling.

Food sources of B_{12}: Liver and other offal, meat, sardines, eggs, cheese and milk. Strict vegetarians (vegans) need B_{12} supplements — especially young children.

In a healthy person, B_{12} from food combines with intrinsic factor, a mucopolysaccharide secreted by the stomach. If this is lacking (usually because of auto-immune disease) B_{12} cannot be absorbed and deficiency will develop.

B_{12}

B_{12} intrinsic factor complex

Intrinsic factor

Folate ● is absorbed throughout the small intestine.

Folate

Liver

B_{12}

Folate

Large amounts of B_{12} are stored in the liver. Body stores of folate amount to only three months' supply.

B_{12}

B_{12} and folate are needed for the manufacture of healthy blood cells in the bone marrow

The B_{12}-intrinsic factor complex is absorbed in the terminal ileum.

B_{12}

Bone

B_{12} Deficiency may develop when intestinal disease causes malabsorption, or if abnormal bacteria in a 'blind loop' or diverticulum of gut compete for available B_{12}.

Folate deficiency may develop:
— if diet is poor during pregnancy, when the body's requirements double.
— during prolonged intravenous feeding.
— if red cell production rises for any reason (eg to replace losses, or in some bone marrow diseases)
— when some drugs are taken — eg phenytoin, methotrexate, co-trimoxazole.

If folate alone is given to someone who also lacks B_{12}, the severe neurological condition of subacute combined degeneration of the cord can develop.

White blood cells (WBCs or leucocytes)

These are important in the body's immune defence.
Red blood cells are all the same, but there are
several varieties of white cells.
They look different, and also work in different ways.

Granulocytes make up about 2/3 of the total number (67%).
They are so called because their lobed nucleus is set in
cytoplasm which contains granules.
Depending on what sort of stain the granules take up on
laboratory testing, granulocytes are divided into
neutrophils, eosinophils and basophils.

Capillary wall

Plasma

Erythrocytes
(red blood cells)

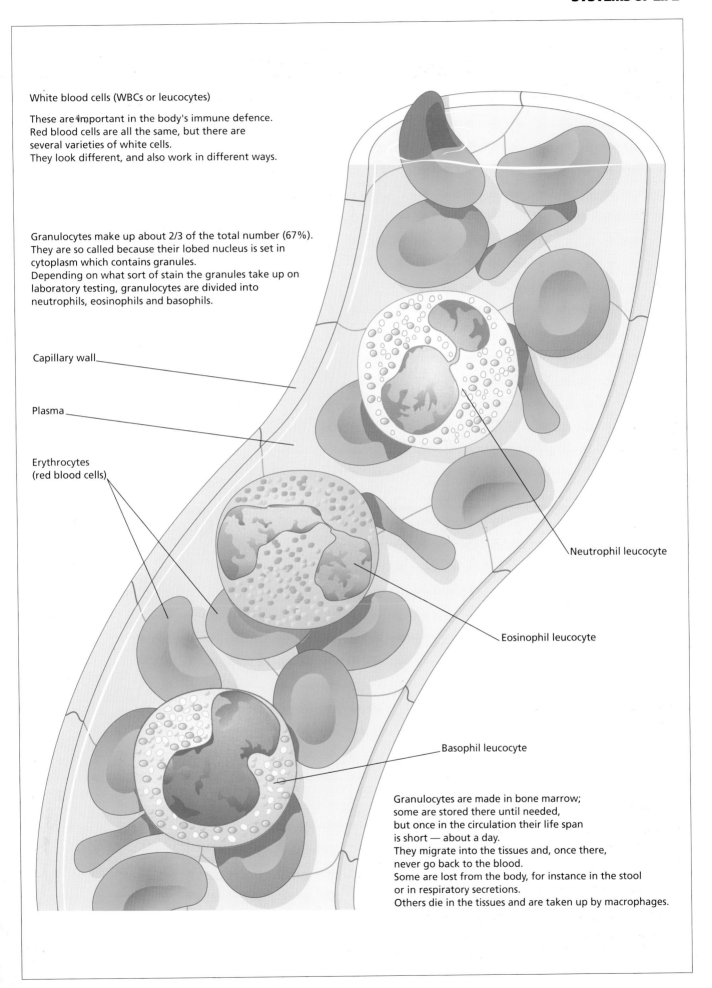

Neutrophil leucocyte

Eosinophil leucocyte

Basophil leucocyte

Granulocytes are made in bone marrow;
some are stored there until needed,
but once in the circulation their life span
is short — about a day.
They migrate into the tissues and, once there,
never go back to the blood.
Some are lost from the body, for instance in the stool
or in respiratory secretions.
Others die in the tissues and are taken up by macrophages.

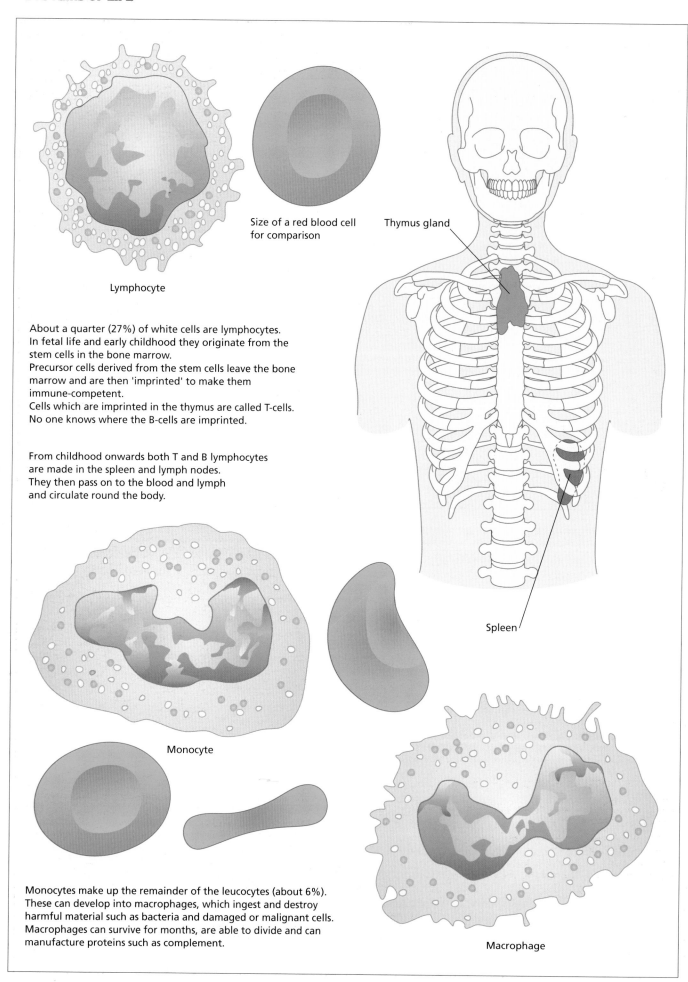

Size of a red blood cell
for comparison

Thymus gland

Lymphocyte

About a quarter (27%) of white cells are lymphocytes.
In fetal life and early childhood they originate from the
stem cells in the bone marrow.
Precursor cells derived from the stem cells leave the bone
marrow and are then 'imprinted' to make them
immune-competent.
Cells which are imprinted in the thymus are called T-cells.
No one knows where the B-cells are imprinted.

From childhood onwards both T and B lymphocytes
are made in the spleen and lymph nodes.
They then pass on to the blood and lymph
and circulate round the body.

Spleen

Monocyte

Monocytes make up the remainder of the leucocytes (about 6%).
These can develop into macrophages, which ingest and destroy
harmful material such as bacteria and damaged or malignant cells.
Macrophages can survive for months, are able to divide and can
manufacture proteins such as complement.

Macrophage

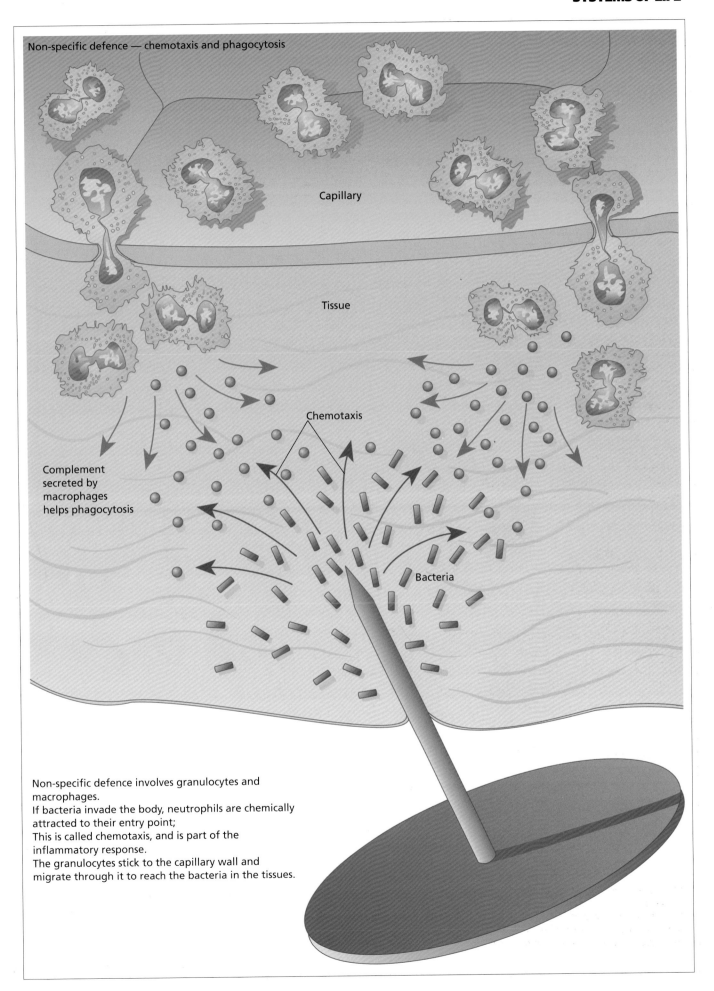

Non-specific defence — chemotaxis and phagocytosis

Capillary

Tissue

Chemotaxis

Complement
secreted by
macrophages
helps phagocytosis

Bacteria

Non-specific defence involves granulocytes and
macrophages.
If bacteria invade the body, neutrophils are chemically
attracted to their entry point;
This is called chemotaxis, and is part of the
inflammatory response.
The granulocytes stick to the capillary wall and
migrate through it to reach the bacteria in the tissues.

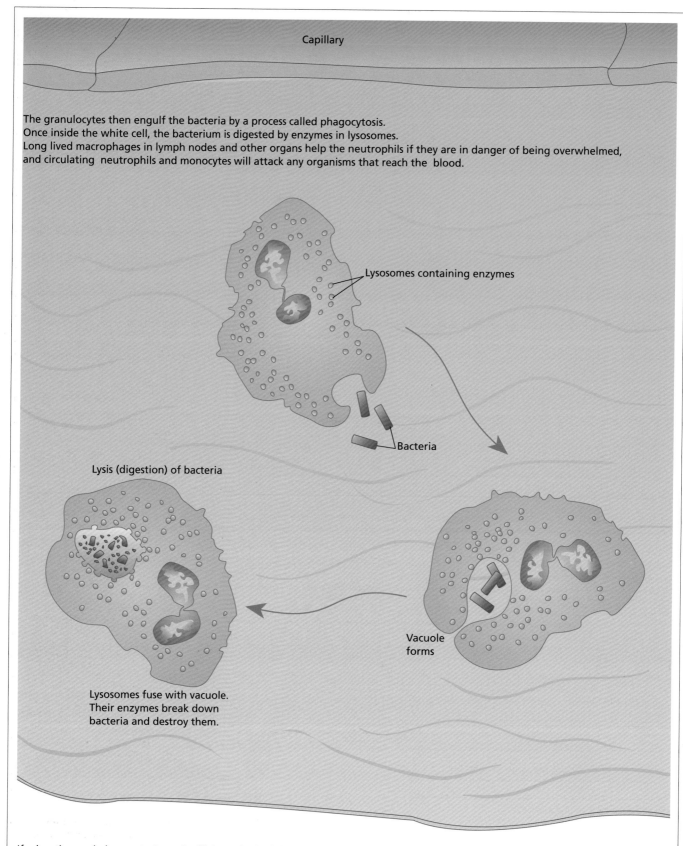

Capillary

The granulocytes then engulf the bacteria by a process called phagocytosis.
Once inside the white cell, the bacterium is digested by enzymes in lysosomes.
Long lived macrophages in lymph nodes and other organs help the neutrophils if they are in danger of being overwhelmed, and circulating neutrophils and monocytes will attack any organisms that reach the blood.

Lysosomes containing enzymes

Bacteria

Lysis (digestion) of bacteria

Vacuole forms

Lysosomes fuse with vacuole.
Their enzymes break down
bacteria and destroy them.

If migration and phagocytosis are inefficient, the body becomes prone to infection.
This happens in people with diabetes, those on steroid therapy and those who abuse alcohol.
Some organisms have 'learned' to oppose the action of neutrophils.
They may do this by:
— preventing phagocytosis
— being impervious to the lysosomal enzymes
— killing the neutrophils
Because of this, there are other back-up lines of defence.

How the different types of white cells develop

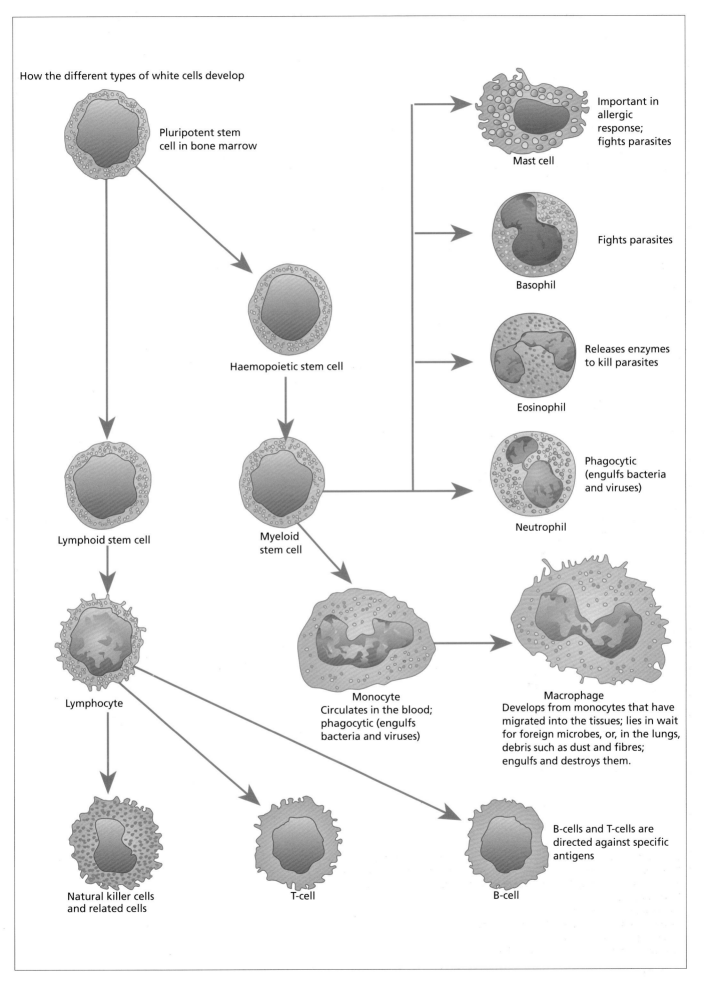

Pluripotent stem cell in bone marrow

Haemopoietic stem cell

Lymphoid stem cell

Myeloid stem cell

Mast cell
Important in allergic response; fights parasites

Basophil
Fights parasites

Eosinophil
Releases enzymes to kill parasites

Neutrophil
Phagocytic (engulfs bacteria and viruses)

Lymphocyte

Monocyte
Circulates in the blood; phagocytic (engulfs bacteria and viruses)

Macrophage
Develops from monocytes that have migrated into the tissues; lies in wait for foreign microbes, or, in the lungs, debris such as dust and fibres; engulfs and destroys them.

Natural killer cells and related cells

T-cell

B-cell
B-cells and T-cells are directed against specific antigens

Specific defence —.(a) Humoral

Around the time of birth, the immune system learns to distinguish between 'self' and 'non-self'.
'Non-self' substances act as antigens and provoke the immune system to produce antibodies against them.
Substances the body recognises as 'self' do not evoke this reaction.

How antibodies are produced

When an antigen such as a bacterium or virus circulates in the body, it is engulfed by macrophages in the spleen and lymph nodes (phagocytosis).

Antigen

Antigens on cell surface

Membrane-bound antibodies

T-helper cell

After being partially broken down, the organisms' remains are then incorporated into part of the macrophage cell wall. They then act as antigens.

Macrophage and T-helper cell stimulate B-cell

Macrophage

B-lymphocytes which encounter these antigens develop into plasma cells which produce the appropriate specific antibody to combat the antigen. Specialised lymphocytes called T-helper cells assist in this process. This is the primary immune response

The plasma cells then divide many times to produce clones of plasma cells, all producing quantities of the same antibody. They also form clones of memory cells.

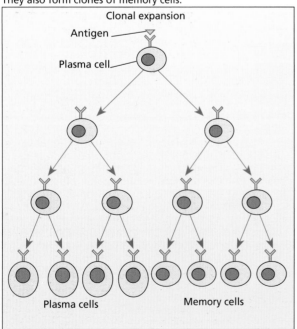

Clonal expansion

Antigen

Plasma cell

Plasma cells   Memory cells

An antigen which has reacted with an antibody is easier for the immune system to dispose of.

Once the body has dealt with an antigen in this way, the production of the appropriate antibody is programmed into its memory cells.

If the body meets the antigen again, large amounts of antibody can be produced very quickly — the secondary response.

Specific defence (b) Cellular
Some organisms cannot be neutralised by antibodies in the specific humoral response.
These include some viruses, *Brucella* bacteria and *Mycobacterium tuberculosis*;
they are countered by the cellular immune response.
This is a slow process, taking about 2 days to reach peak efficiency;
it is therefore sometimes called the delayed immune response.

How the cellular response happens

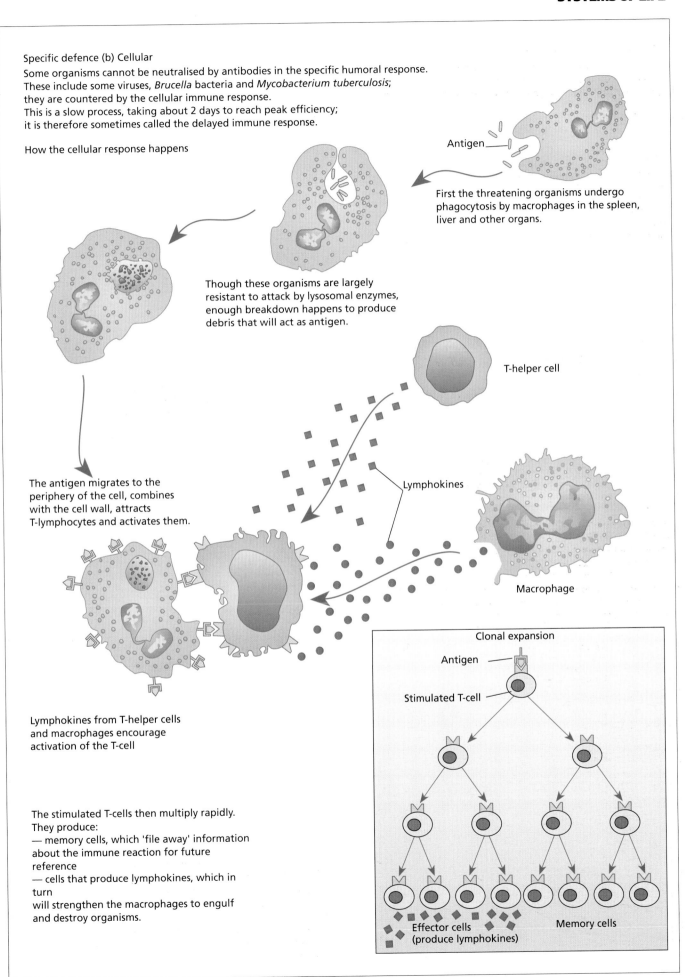

Antigen

First the threatening organisms undergo phagocytosis by macrophages in the spleen, liver and other organs.

Though these organisms are largely resistant to attack by lysosomal enzymes, enough breakdown happens to produce debris that will act as antigen.

T-helper cell

The antigen migrates to the periphery of the cell, combines with the cell wall, attracts T-lymphocytes and activates them.

Lymphokines

Macrophage

Lymphokines from T-helper cells and macrophages encourage activation of the T-cell

The stimulated T-cells then multiply rapidly.
They produce:
— memory cells, which 'file away' information about the immune reaction for future reference
— cells that produce lymphokines, which in turn
will strengthen the macrophages to engulf and destroy organisms.

Clonal expansion

Antigen

Stimulated T-cell

Effector cells
(produce lymphokines)

Memory cells

Immunisation

The bacteria and viruses that cause illness are among the 'non-self' substances that elicit an antibody response.
When the body first meets bacteria or viruses and becomes ill, antibodies are gradually produced to put the invader out of action.
This 'primary' response takes a little time, but is usually sufficient to enable the body to overcome the infection
and recover from the illness.
Meanwhile, though, the infection may have caused considerable tissue damage,
and some patients will be overwhelmed by it and will die.

Artificial immunity

If the body can be exposed to an antigen under carefully controlled conditions,
it is possible to activate its immunological memory without an illness developing.
On a second encounter with the antigen, the body will produce a rapid secondary response.
Producing immunity without the need for an illness is the basis of immunisation techniques.

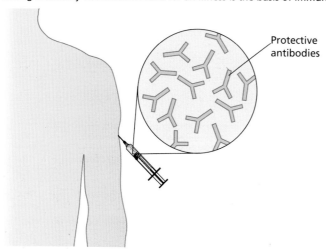

Protective antibodies

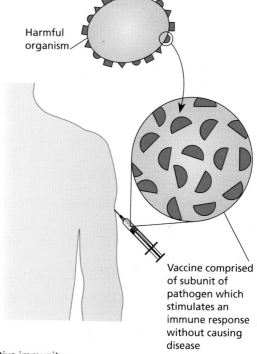

Harmful organism

Vaccine comprised of subunit of pathogen which stimulates an immune response without causing disease

Passive immunity

This involves injecting a patient with ' ready-made' antibodies as human immunoglobulin;
it produces immediate but short-lived protection (about four weeks).
Two types are used:
— human normal immunoglobulin (HNIG) from pooled donor plasma.
This is given to immunosuppressed children who have been exposed to measles, for instance, and to prevent exposed people from developing hepatitis A.
— specific immunoglobulins for tetanus, hepatitis B, rabies and varicella/zoster.
These are obtained selectively from people with high antibody titres because they are convalescing from the disease concerned, or have recently been immunised against it.

Active immunity

This is produced using organisms that have been treated so that they will induce an antibody response without causing disease.

This can be done with:
— live ,attenuated (ie weakened) organisms, as in measles, mumps and rubella and in the oral poliomyelitis vaccine.
— dead organisms, as in whooping cough and typhoid vaccines.
— parts of the organism: tetanus and diphtheria toxoids are the inactivated poisons of the organisms.

The body's 'immunological memory' means that if the same organism is encountered a second time, antibody production can start at once and in much greater quantities(secondary response).

The antibodies are usually able to neutralise the antigen so quickly that the person may not become ill at all.

In other words, immunisation (or surviving a first attack from the organism) means a second encounter will no longer make the person ill:he/she is immune to it.

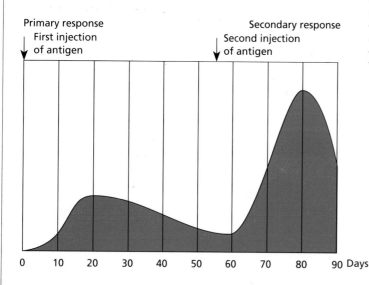

Primary response
First injection of antigen

Secondary response
Second injection of antigen

0 10 20 30 40 50 60 70 80 90 Days

Plasma
This is the fluid medium in which blood cells float.
Its volume is about 3 litres in men and 2.5 litres in women.

It consists of:
— water
— inorganic ions, predominantly sodium, chloride and bicarbonate
— plasma proteins — albumin, fibrinogen and globulins.

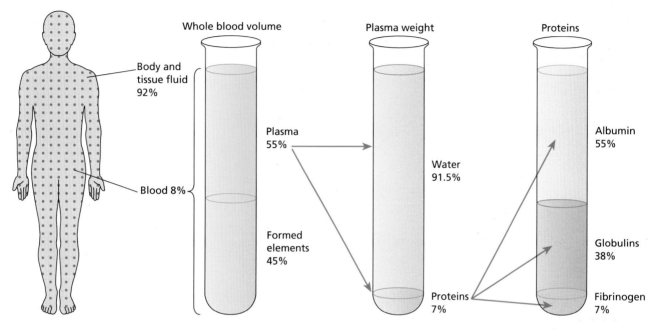

Whole blood volume

Body and tissue fluid 92%

Blood 8%

Plasma 55%

Formed elements 45%

Plasma weight

Water 91.5%

Proteins 7%

Proteins

Albumin 55%

Globulins 38%

Fibrinogen 7%

Functions of plasma proteins
Plasma proteins — act as carriers for substances such as bilirubin and hormones
— exert colloid osmotic pressure to keep fluid in the circulation, rather than leaking out into the tissues as oedema
— function as antibodies
— act as clotting factors
— form a protein reserve, which can used by the body during starvation
— buffer plasma, correcting acid-base balance
— function as enzymes.

Distribution of body water.
Most is inside cells (ICF)
ECF includes plasma, fluid film between cells (interstitial fluid)
and body fluids such as digestive juices, joint fluids and CSF.

ECF (extra cellular fluid 12 litres — 27%)

Interstitial fluid and other body fluids (6.5 litres)

Plasma (5.5 litres)

ICF (intracellular fluid 33 litres — 73%)

Classification of plasma proteins (simplified)

Plasma proteins can be separated by electrophoresis into albumin, $\alpha 1$, $\alpha 2$, β and γ globulins.

The protein fractionation pattern alters in various disease states, so plasma protein electrophoresis may be important in diagnosis.

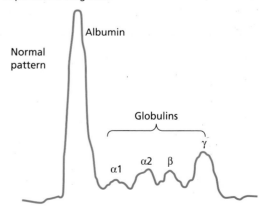

Albumin

Normal pattern

Globulins

$\alpha 1$ $\alpha 2$ β γ

Plasma osmotic pressure helps to keep fluid within blood capillaries.
It is opposed by the hydrostatic pressure of the blood, tending to force fluid out into the tissues.
In health an overall balance is maintained, but a rise in hydrostatic pressure or a fall in osmotic pressure can lead to oedema.

Capillary loop under normal circumstances

Arterial end

Direction of blood flow

Venous end

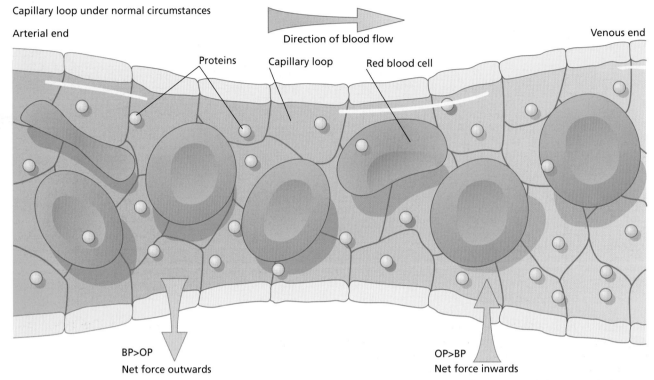

Proteins   Capillary loop   Red blood cell

BP>OP

Net force outwards

OP>BP

Net force inwards

At the arterial end, the hydrostatic pressure (BP) of the plasma exceeds its osmotic pressure (OP), so fluid tends to pass outwards into the tissues.

At the venous end the reverse is the case.

Capillary loop of someone in heart failure

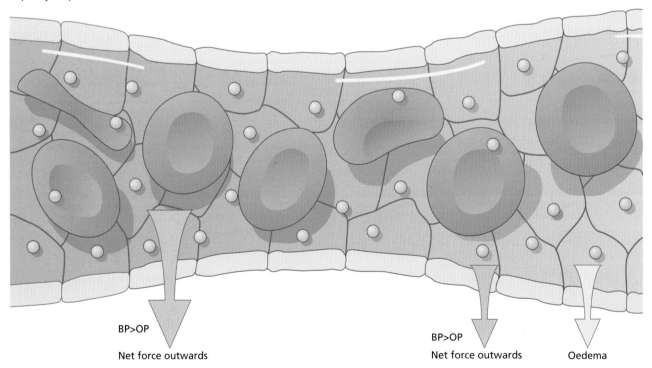

BP>OP

Net force outwards

BP>OP

Net force outwards

Oedema

Plasma volume increases because of salt and water retention.
Hydrostatic pressure rises on the venous side because of the failing heart, and is highest in dependent areas e.g. ankles.
Oedema results, as fluid passes out into the tissues.

How oedema is produced in low-protein states e.g. nephrotic syndrome, starvation

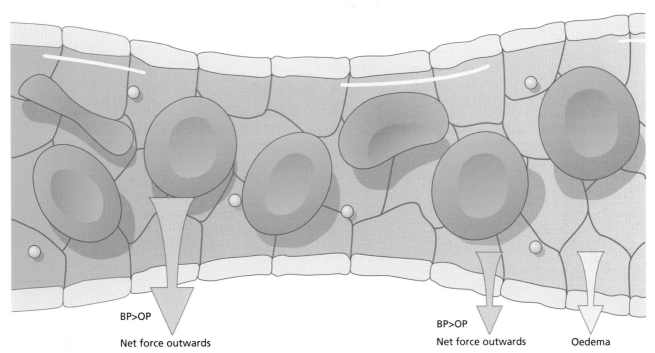

BP>OP

Net force outwards

BP>OP

Net force outwards   Oedema

When protein is low, there is less osmotic pressure to 'suck' fluid into the capillaries.
Though hydrostatic pressure may be normal, it may exceed opposing osmotic pressure,
so fluid is forced out into the tissues, causing oedema.

How inflammation produces local swelling

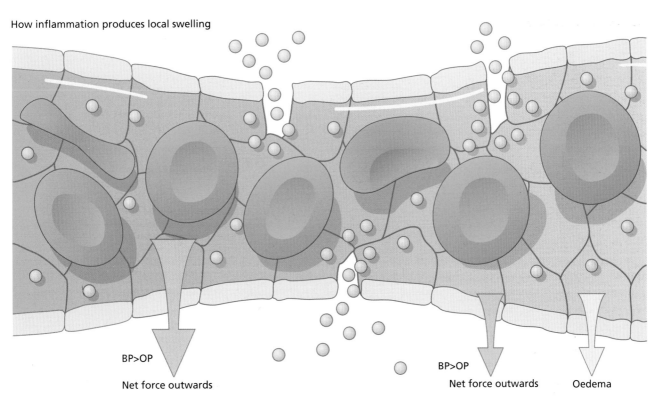

BP>OP

Net force outwards

BP>OP

Net force outwards   Oedema

Inflammation makes it easier for proteins and cells to leak out into the tissues.
Fluid follows the proteins and produces local swelling
— e.g. round an infected wound.

Haematocrit (packed cell volume or PCV)
If blood is centrifuged, the red cells, white cells and platelets separate from the plasma.
Nearly all the spun down deposit consists of red cells; the white cells and platelets form a thin 'buffy coat.

Plasma

Red cells

The fraction $\dfrac{\text{red cells}}{\text{plasma}}$

is called the haematocrit or packed cell volume.

In men the normal value is 0.4 — 0.54; in women it is 0.37 — 0.49.

This reading is of diagnostic importance as it is affected by:
— changes in plasma volume
— changes in red cell mass.

A

Normally hydrated, non-anaemic person — centrifuged blood sample

'Buffy coat'

PCV (volume of packed red cells)
— 0.45 of tube
—haematocrit (Hct) = 0.45

A2 Patient A dehydrated

Red cell volume unchanged; plasma volume reduced.
Percentage of tube occupied by red cells is higher
Hct (PCV) — 0.6

B Normally hydrated but anaemic person

Number of red cells reduced

Haematocrit reduced

Hct (PCV) 0.35

B2 Patient B dehydrated

Plasma volume reduced, but because of anaemia, *proportion* of red cells to plasma may appear normal

PCV (Hct) 0.45 — appears normal because patient has 2 things wrong

Blood groups and transfusion

There are two main blood grouping systems in humans: The ABO system and the Rhesus system.

The Rhesus system

About 85% people have the Rhesus antigen D on their red cells, and are thus said to be Rhesus positive.
They do not make anti-D antibodies.
The red cells of Rhesus negative people lack the D antigen.
Rhesus negative people can make anti-D antibodies, but only do so if they have been sensitised to D.

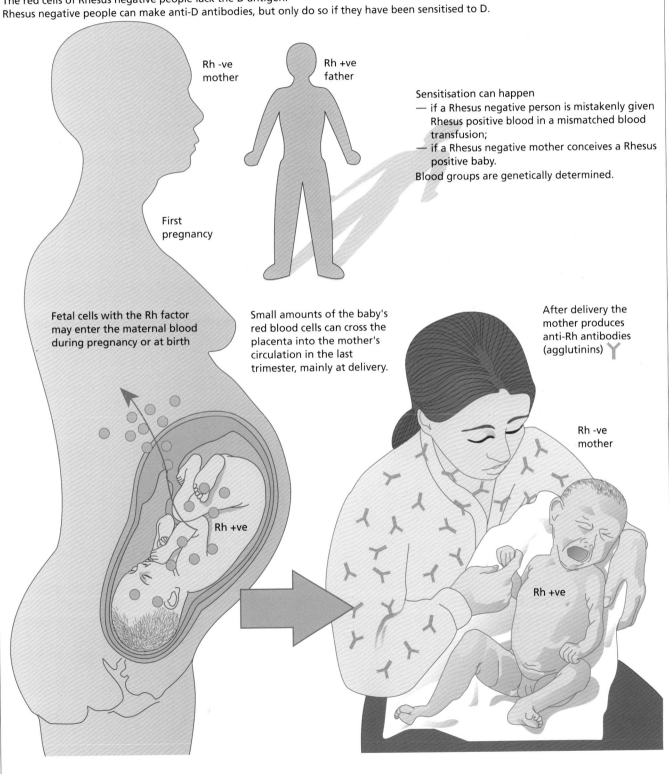

Rh -ve
mother

Rh +ve
father

Sensitisation can happen
— if a Rhesus negative person is mistakenly given Rhesus positive blood in a mismatched blood transfusion;
— if a Rhesus negative mother conceives a Rhesus positive baby.
Blood groups are genetically determined.

First
pregnancy

Fetal cells with the Rh factor may enter the maternal blood during pregnancy or at birth

Small amounts of the baby's red blood cells can cross the placenta into the mother's circulation in the last trimester, mainly at delivery.

After delivery the mother produces anti-Rh antibodies (agglutinins)

Rh -ve
mother

Rh +ve

Rh +ve

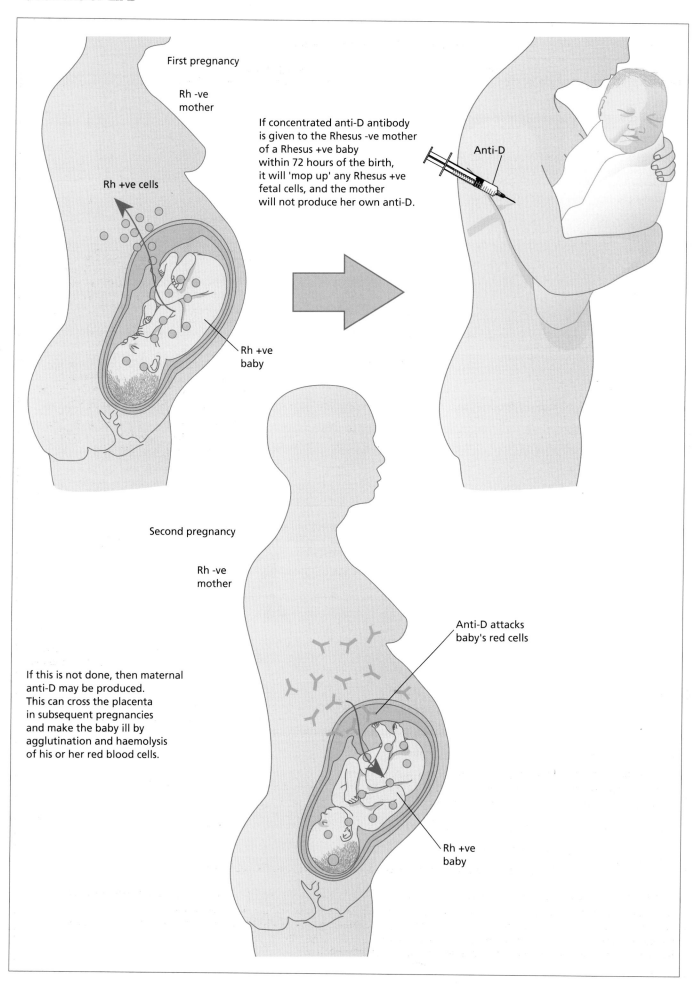

First pregnancy

Rh -ve
mother

Rh +ve cells

If concentrated anti-D antibody
is given to the Rhesus -ve mother
of a Rhesus +ve baby
within 72 hours of the birth,
it will 'mop up' any Rhesus +ve
fetal cells, and the mother
will not produce her own anti-D.

Anti-D

Rh +ve
baby

Second pregnancy

Rh -ve
mother

Anti-D attacks
baby's red cells

If this is not done, then maternal
anti-D may be produced.
This can cross the placenta
in subsequent pregnancies
and make the baby ill by
agglutination and haemolysis
of his or her red blood cells.

Rh +ve
baby

This can cause the serious condition of Rhesus haemolytic disease of the newborn:

— hydrops fetalis; severe anaemia, oedema, jaundice and enlarged liver and spleen;

— icterus gravis neonatorum (severe jaundice of the newborn):

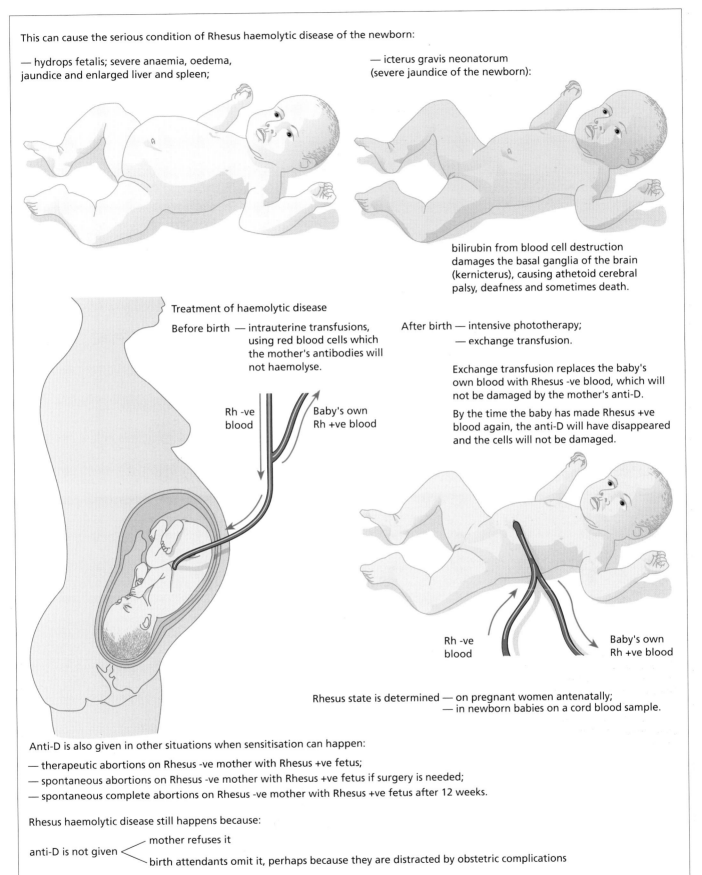

bilirubin from blood cell destruction damages the basal ganglia of the brain (kernicterus), causing athetoid cerebral palsy, deafness and sometimes death.

Treatment of haemolytic disease

Before birth — intrauterine transfusions, using red blood cells which the mother's antibodies will not haemolyse.

After birth — intensive phototherapy;
— exchange transfusion.

Exchange transfusion replaces the baby's own blood with Rhesus -ve blood, which will not be damaged by the mother's anti-D.

By the time the baby has made Rhesus +ve blood again, the anti-D will have disappeared and the cells will not be damaged.

Rh -ve blood

Baby's own Rh +ve blood

Rh -ve blood

Baby's own Rh +ve blood

Rhesus state is determined — on pregnant women antenatally;
— in newborn babies on a cord blood sample.

Anti-D is also given in other situations when sensitisation can happen:

— therapeutic abortions on Rhesus -ve mother with Rhesus +ve fetus;
— spontaneous abortions on Rhesus -ve mother with Rhesus +ve fetus if surgery is needed;
— spontaneous complete abortions on Rhesus -ve mother with Rhesus +ve fetus after 12 weeks.

Rhesus haemolytic disease still happens because:

anti-D is not given ⟨ mother refuses it
birth attendants omit it, perhaps because they are distracted by obstetric complications

Significant amounts of anti-D usually become apparent in the last trimester of the second pregnancy, ie, the first baby is spared.
Some Rhesus negative mothers develop antibodies even in their first pregnancy, so their first baby is affected.
This can be prevented by giving anti-D during the first pregnancy, but this may be difficult to achieve if anti-D is in short supply.
Haemolytic disease of the newborn can also be caused by other red cell antibodies,
but this is much less common and many cases are too mild to need treatment.

Inheritance of Rhesus system

Rhesus +ve is dominant to Rhesus -ve:
if a baby receives a Rhesus +ve gene from one parent (D) and a Rhesus -ve one (d) from the other,
it will be heterozygous Rhesus +ve (Dd).
Homozygous Rhesus +ve (D) from each parent is DD.
Homozygous Rh -ve (d from each parent) is dd.

If a mother is Rh -ve and the father Rh +ve — homozygous

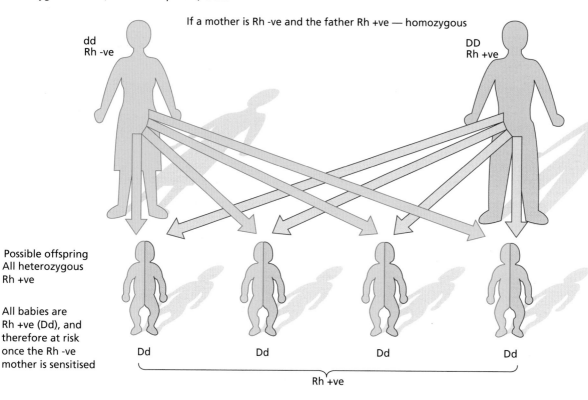

dd
Rh -ve

DD
Rh +ve

Possible offspring
All heterozygous
Rh +ve

All babies are
Rh +ve (Dd), and
therefore at risk
once the Rh -ve
mother is sensitised

Dd   Dd   Dd   Dd

Rh +ve

If a mother is Rh -ve and the father heterozygous Rh +ve:

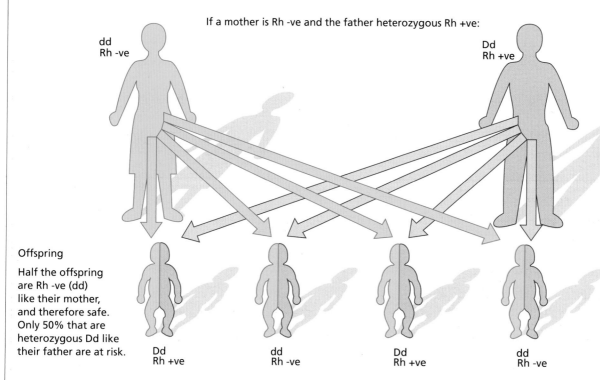

dd
Rh -ve

Dd
Rh +ve

Offspring

Half the offspring
are Rh -ve (dd)
like their mother,
and therefore safe.
Only 50% that are
heterozygous Dd like
their father are at risk.

Dd   dd   Dd   dd
Rh +ve   Rh -ve   Rh +ve   Rh -ve

ABO system

This depends on:
— what polysaccharide agglutinogens are found on the person's red blood cells (RBCs);
— what, if any, agglutinin antibodies (mainly IgM) are present in the person's serum.

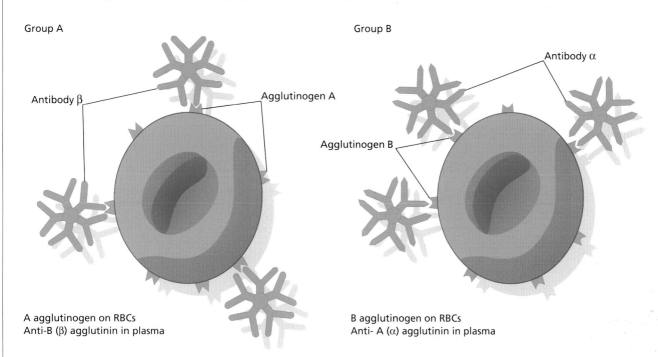

Group A

Antibody β — Agglutinogen A

A agglutinogen on RBCs
Anti-B (β) agglutinin in plasma

Group B

Antibody α

Agglutinogen B

B agglutinogen on RBCs
Anti- A (α) agglutinin in plasma

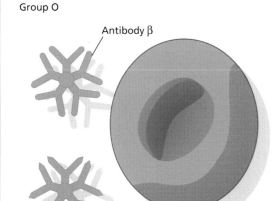

Group O

Antibody β

Antibody α

No agglutinogen on RBCs
Anti-A (α) and anti-B (β) agglutinin in plasma

Group AB

Agglutinogen A

Agglutinogen B

A and B agglutinogen on RBCs
No agglutinins in plasma

If by accident the cells with agglutinogen meet the corresponding agglutinin,
they agglutinate and haemolyse — that is, clump together and burst.
This can happen in a mismatched blood transfusion.
To avoid this, blood for transfusion is carefully tested for compatibility with the recipient's blood before it is used.
The donor cells are tested against the recipient's plasma,
as the agglutinins in the donor's plasma are so much diluted by the recipient's blood that they have little effect.

Principles of testing
Washed donor cells are mixed on a slide with plasma from a known group.
For instance, in the specimens below, Group A plasma contains anti-B, and Group B contains anti-A agglutinins.

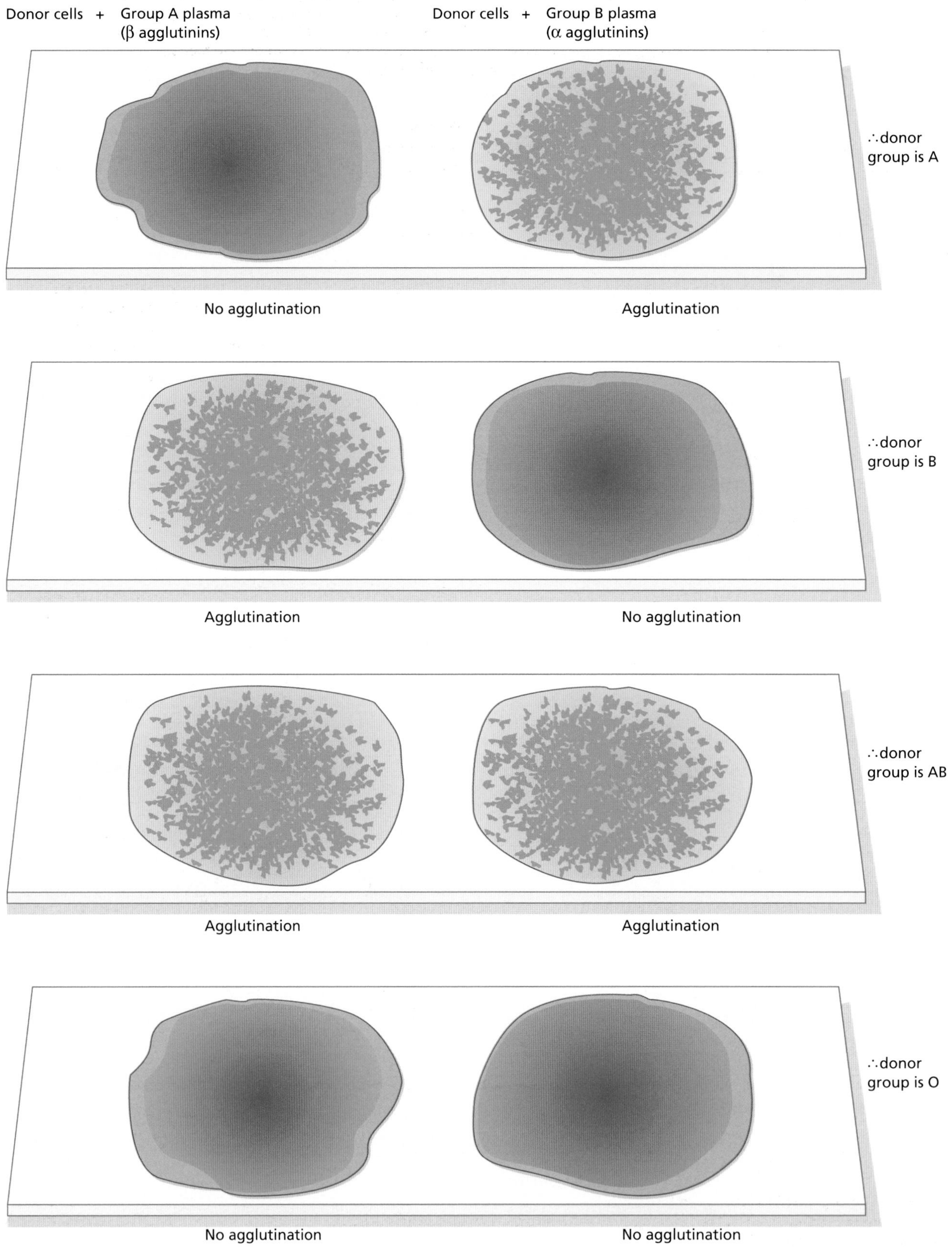

Donor cells + Group A plasma
(β agglutinins)

Donor cells + Group B plasma
(α agglutinins)

∴donor group is A

No agglutination

Agglutination

∴donor group is B

Agglutination

No agglutination

∴donor group is AB

Agglutination

Agglutination

∴donor group is O

No agglutination

No agglutination

Blood donation and transfusion

This should not — cause ill effects in donor;
— transmit disease to recipient.

To avoid anaemia from high iron demands of early adolescence, and risk of precipitating cardiovascular problems in later life, donors should be over 18 and under 60 (that is, first-time donors — regular donors in good health may be older).
To avoid transmission of disease, donors should be in good health. Blood is tested for hepatitis B and C, syphilis and HIV.
(Because HIV may be transmitted before testing is positive, people at high risk are not allowed to donate blood.)
In certain circumstances, tests are also performed for malaria and cytomegalovirus.
Many different blood components can be given to correct deficiencies.

Giving red cells safely

Red cells are given to improve the delivery of oxygen to the tissues in a short time,
e.g., to replace acute blood loss through accident or surgery, before an operation, or occasionally to treat anaemia or in renal failure.

What can go wrong

Immediate problems

Circulatory overload

— especially risky in older people with heart disease who are transfused too rapidly.
Prevent by — monitoring CVP
— transfusing slowly.

Haemolytic reactions

— produce fever, tachycardia, loin pain, restlessness, rigors, vomiting, diarrhoea, headache, difficulty in breathing, hypotension and shock. This can progress to acute renal failure and disseminated intravascular coagulation.

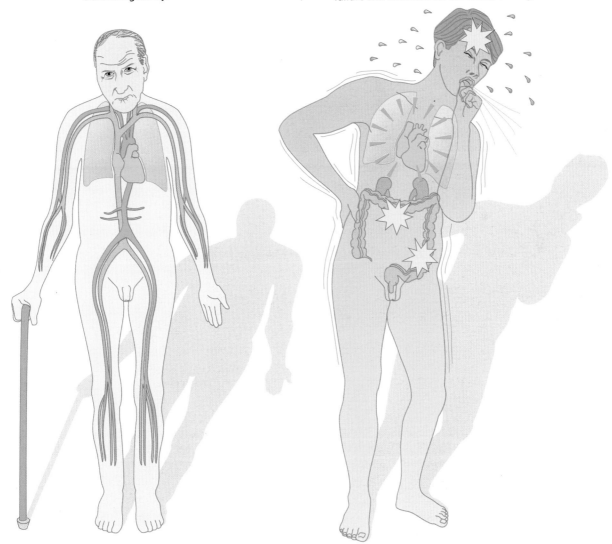

Hyperkalaemia (high blood potassium)
— prevent by storing blood at correct temperature before use and using within 8 hours;
— monitor potassium level.

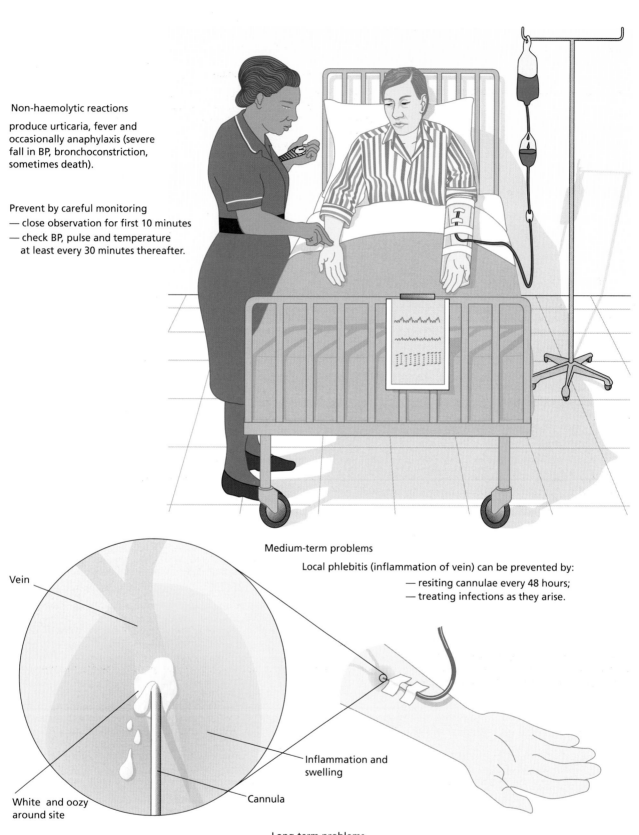

Non-haemolytic reactions produce urticaria, fever and occasionally anaphylaxis (severe fall in BP, bronchoconstriction, sometimes death).

Prevent by careful monitoring
— close observation for first 10 minutes
— check BP, pulse and temperature at least every 30 minutes thereafter.

Medium-term problems

Local phlebitis (inflammation of vein) can be prevented by:
— resiting cannulae every 48 hours;
— treating infections as they arise.

Vein

White and oozy around site

Cannula

Inflammation and swelling

Long-term problems

Iron overload Avoid in people needing repeated transfusions by chelation with desferrioxamine. This binds iron, so it can be excreted harmlessly in the urine.

Deaths from mismatched transfusions are usually due to mistakes in identification procedures, not to faults in cross-matching. To avoid this, two people should check that the transfusion form, the compatibility labels, the labels on the blood, the patient's notes and the patient's wristband all agree.

Haemostasis — how blood flow stops after injury

This happens because of interactions between: — platelets (thrombocytes) in the blood.
These are produced in the bone marrow by megakaryocytes.
They circulate for 7-14 days before being destroyed in the spleen.
— blood vessels
— plasma and tissue factors.

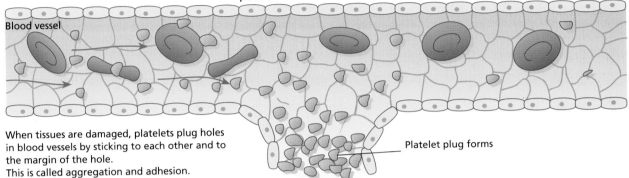

Blood vessel

When tissues are damaged, platelets plug holes
in blood vessels by sticking to each other and to
the margin of the hole.
This is called aggregation and adhesion.

Platelet plug forms

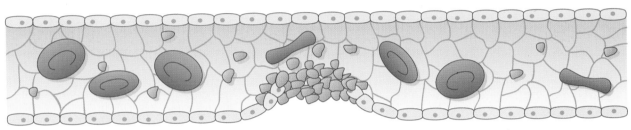

The damaged blood vessels constrict at the edges and roll inwards, making the hole smaller and easier to seal.
This process is helped by serotonin and other factors released from platelets.

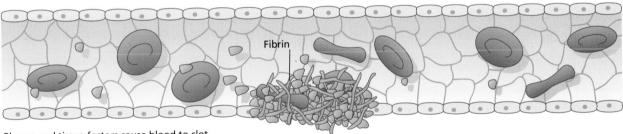

Fibrin

Plasma and tissue factors cause blood to clot.
Soluble fibrinogen changes to tough, insoluble threads of fibrin, reinforcing the platelet plug and further strengthening the clot by
trapping platelets and red cells in their tangled fibres.

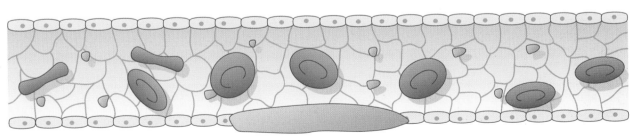

Contractile proteins in the platelets help the clot to retract.
Fibroblasts move in, and connective tissue forms (organisation).
Finally, scar tissue may form, the lining endothelium of blood vessels regenerates and the tissues are healed.

How blood clots
Clotting factors are present in the blood all the time, but they only function as enzymes once they are activated.
They are known as:

I Fibrinogen	VII Proconvertin
II Prothrombin	VIII Anti-haemophilic factor (AHF), anti-haemophilia globulin (AHG)
III Thromboplastin	IX Christmas factor, plasma thromboplastin component (PTC)
IV Calcium	X Stuart-Prower factor
V Proaccelerin	XI Plasma thromboplastin antecedent (PTA)
VI (Synonym no longer used)	XII Hageman factor, contact factor
	XIII Fibrin stabilising factor

Two systems can activate a final common pathway.
Intrinsic system: this deals with minor defects in the endothelial lining of the blood vessels.

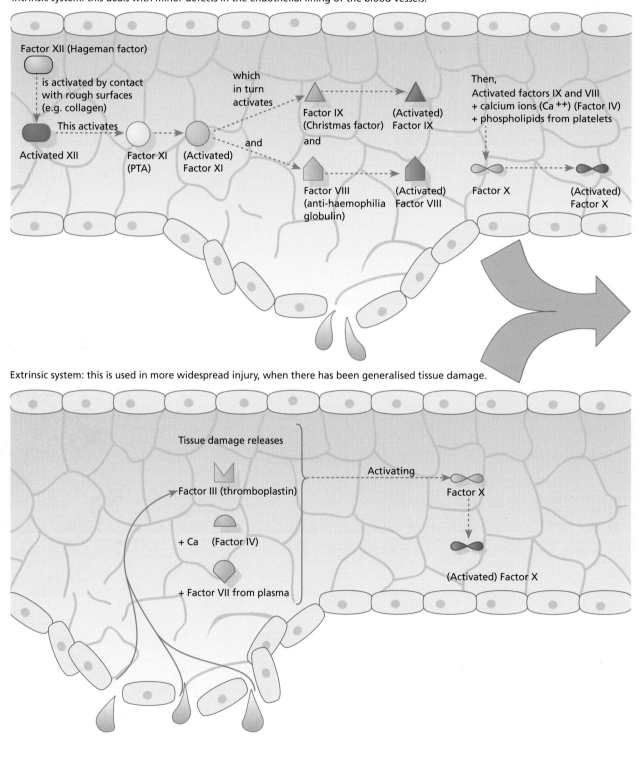

Extrinsic system: this is used in more widespread injury, when there has been generalised tissue damage.

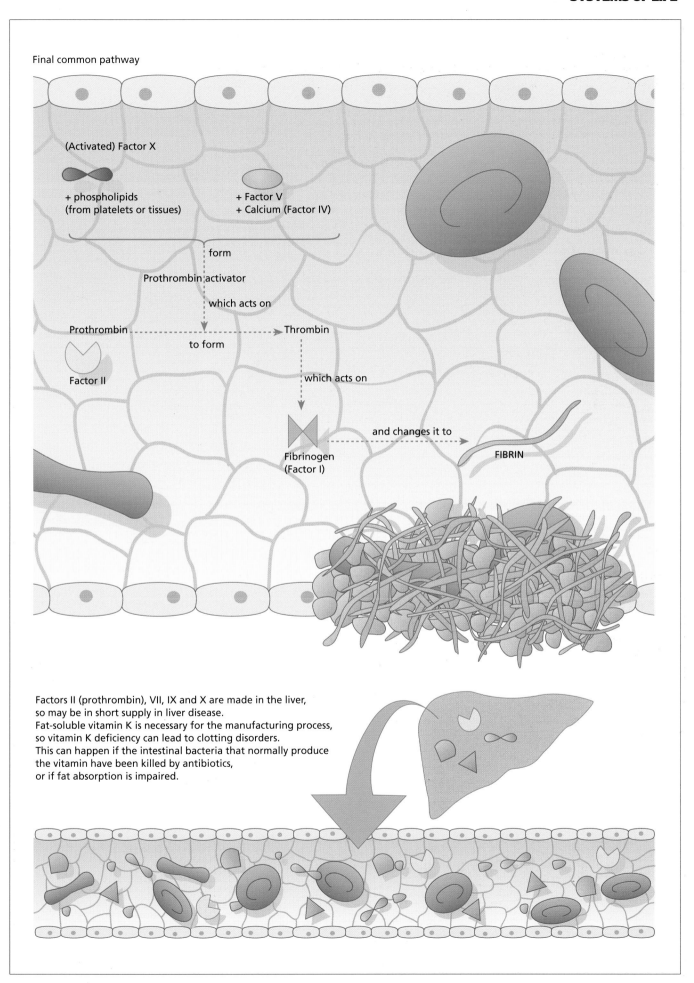

Final common pathway

(Activated) Factor X

+ phospholipids
(from platelets or tissues)

+ Factor V
+ Calcium (Factor IV)

form

Prothrombin activator

which acts on

Prothrombin

Factor II

to form

Thrombin

which acts on

Fibrinogen
(Factor I)

and changes it to

FIBRIN

Factors II (prothrombin), VII, IX and X are made in the liver,
so may be in short supply in liver disease.
Fat-soluble vitamin K is necessary for the manufacturing process,
so vitamin K deficiency can lead to clotting disorders.
This can happen if the intestinal bacteria that normally produce
the vitamin have been killed by antibiotics,
or if fat absorption is impaired.

Fibrinolysis
Once clotting has gone far enough to halt blood loss and to provide a scaffolding for the healing process, it must be stopped. Further thrombosis would be dangerous, as the blocked blood vessels could no longer supply the necessary blood to the tissues.

Inactive plasminogen can be activated to plasma in a number of different ways.
Some substances that do this are used in treatment called thrombolysis
— e.g. dissolving freshly formed clots in the coronary arteries.

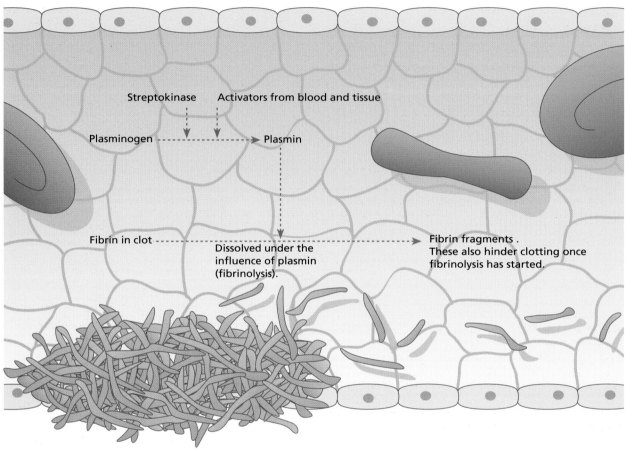

Streptokinase   Activators from blood and tissue

Plasminogen - - - - - - - - - - → Plasmin

Fibrin in clot - - - - - - - - - - - - -
                    Dissolved under the
                    influence of plasmin
                    (fibrinolysis).

Fibrin fragments .
These also hinder clotting once
fibrinolysis has started.

Another agent preventing excess clotting is antithrombin 3.

This is a plasma protein which combines with clotting factors to form inactive complexes and thus put them out of action.

In health, the factors producing clots and the factors dissolving them must be carefully balanced.
Otherwise, the body will be threatened either by haemorrhage or by loss of blood supply through clotted, blocked vessels.

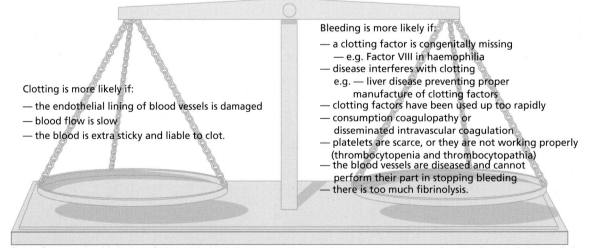

Clotting is more likely if:

— the endothelial lining of blood vessels is damaged
— blood flow is slow
— the blood is extra sticky and liable to clot.

Bleeding is more likely if:

— a clotting factor is congenitally missing
   — e.g. Factor VIII in haemophilia
— disease interferes with clotting
   e.g. — liver disease preventing proper
        manufacture of clotting factors
— clotting factors have been used up too rapidly
— consumption coagulopathy or
   disseminated intravascular coagulation
— platelets are scarce, or they are not working properly
   (thrombocytopenia and thrombocytopathia)
— the blood vessels are diseased and cannot
   perform their part in stopping bleeding
— there is too much fibrinolysis.

When illness threatens health by interfering with this balance, treatment with appropriate drugs or the transfusion of clotting factors can restore equilibrium.

The lymphatic system

The lymphatic system consists of:

— thin-walled lymphatic vessels that empty into veins

— lymph nodes, found in groups along blood vessels

— accessory organs: tonsils and adenoids, thymus, spleen.

The functions of the lymphatic system are:

— to return substances such as proteins to the circulation
  when they have leaked out of blood vessels

— to help in bodily defence, by producing lymphocytes and antibodies
  and filtering lymph to remove infective matter and malignant cells

— to absorb fat from the intestine and distribute it to the tissues.

The right lymphatic duct drains the right arm and the right side of
the head, neck and chest.
It opens into the venous system where the right internal jugular
and right subclavian veins meet.

The thoracic duct starts as the cisterna chyli opposite the second
lumbar vertebra.
It runs upwards through the abdomen and chest to empty into the
veins where the left internal jugular joins the left subclavian.
The thoracic duct carries lymph from the legs, pelvis, abdomen,
left arm and left side of the head, neck and chest.

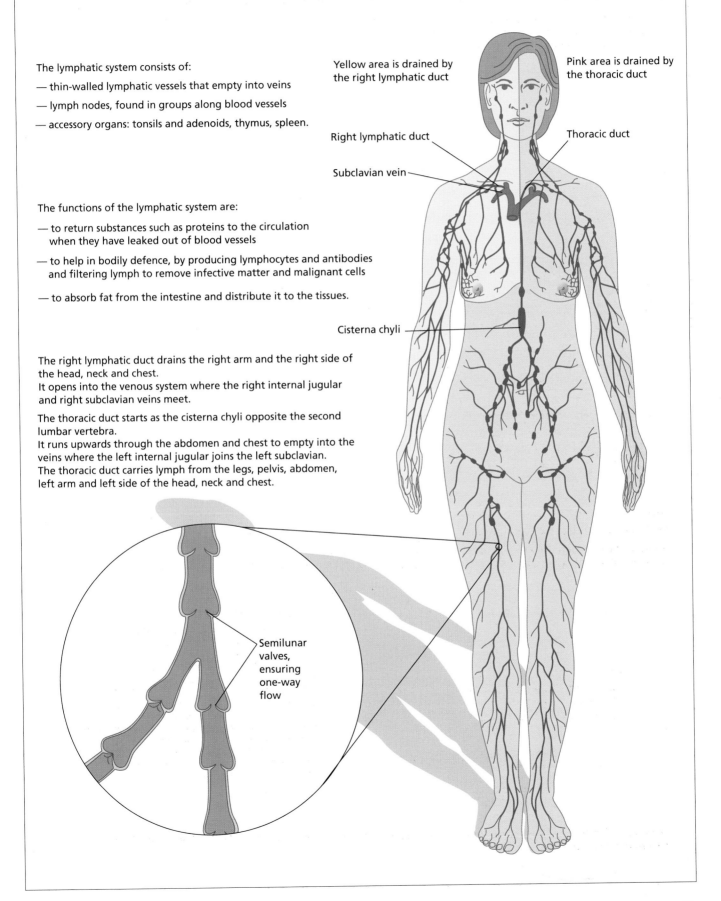

Yellow area is drained by
the right lymphatic duct

Pink area is drained by
the thoracic duct

Right lymphatic duct

Thoracic duct

Subclavian vein

Cisterna chyli

Semilunar
valves,
ensuring
one-way
flow

How the circulation of blood and lymph are connected

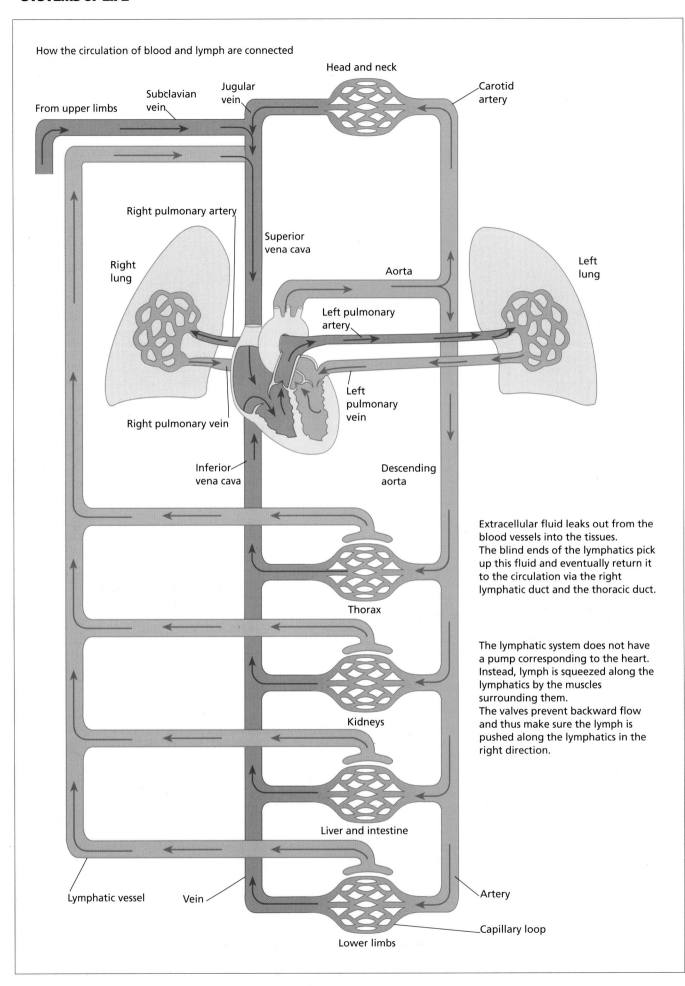

Extracellular fluid leaks out from the blood vessels into the tissues.
The blind ends of the lymphatics pick up this fluid and eventually return it to the circulation via the right lymphatic duct and the thoracic duct.

The lymphatic system does not have a pump corresponding to the heart. Instead, lymph is squeezed along the lymphatics by the muscles surrounding them.
The valves prevent backward flow and thus make sure the lymph is pushed along the lymphatics in the right direction.

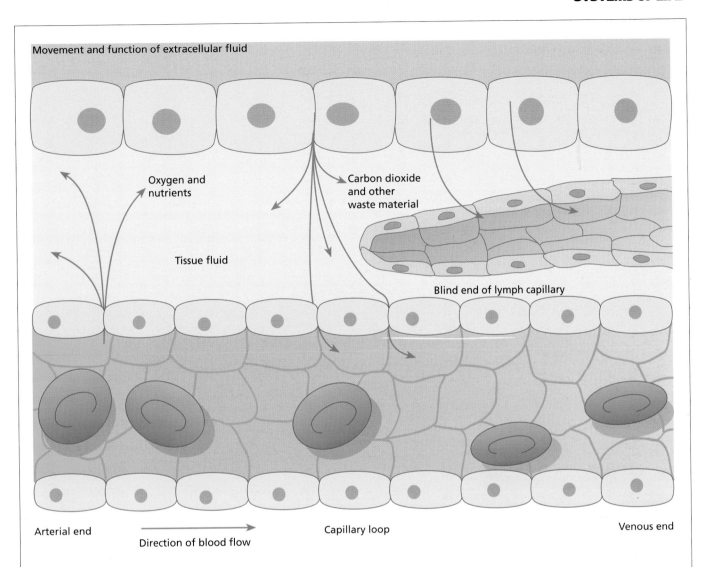

Movement and function of extracellular fluid

Oxygen and nutrients

Carbon dioxide and other waste material

Tissue fluid

Blind end of lymph capillary

Arterial end

Direction of blood flow

Capillary loop

Venous end

The extracellular fluid serves a very important function, as it is the vital last link in the chain carrying oxygen and nutrients from the outside of the body to the tissues themselves.
It then takes carbon dioxide and other waste products back into the circulation.
Some of the returning fluid seeps back into the venules, but the rest is collected and returned by the lymphatics.

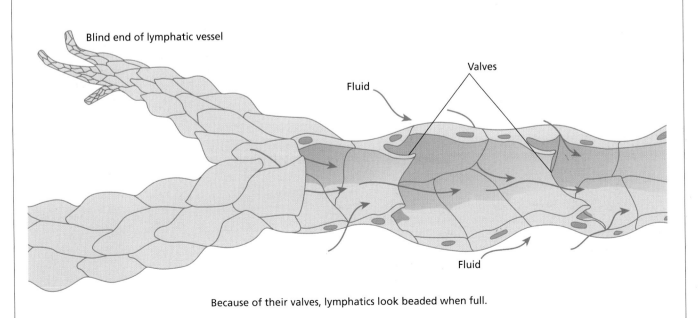

Blind end of lymphatic vessel

Valves

Fluid

Fluid

Because of their valves, lymphatics look beaded when full.

Solid organs of the lymphatic system

A lymph node

Lymph passes through several groups of lymph nodes before it reaches the blood. It enters the node by several vessels and leaves by one or two.

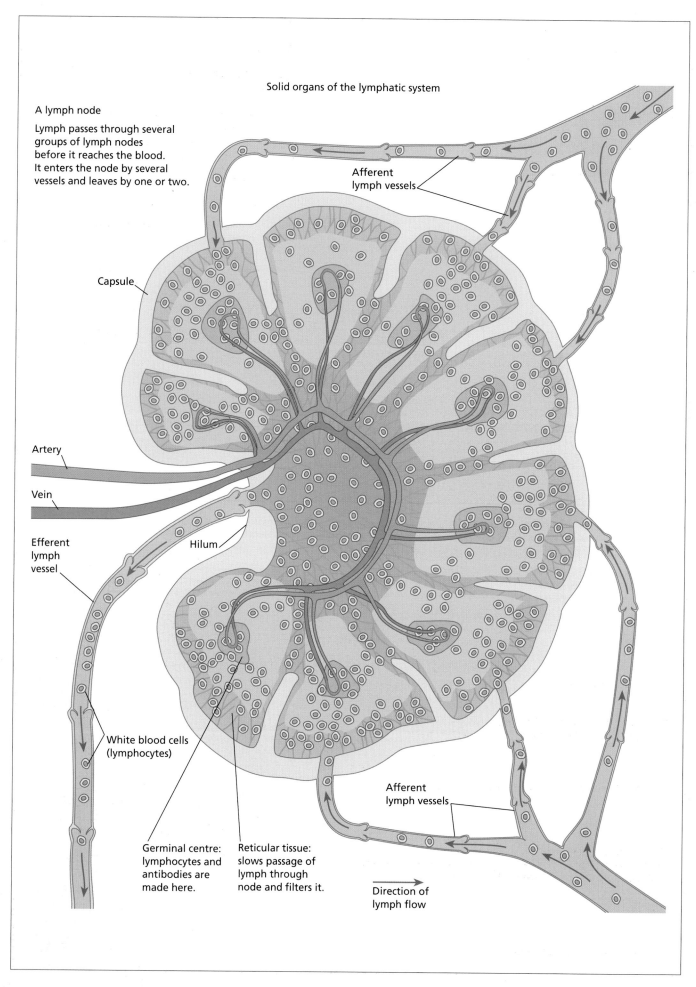

Afferent lymph vessels

Capsule

Artery

Vein

Efferent lymph vessel

Hilum

White blood cells (lymphocytes)

Germinal centre: lymphocytes and antibodies are made here.

Reticular tissue: slows passage of lymph through node and filters it.

Afferent lymph vessels

Direction of lymph flow

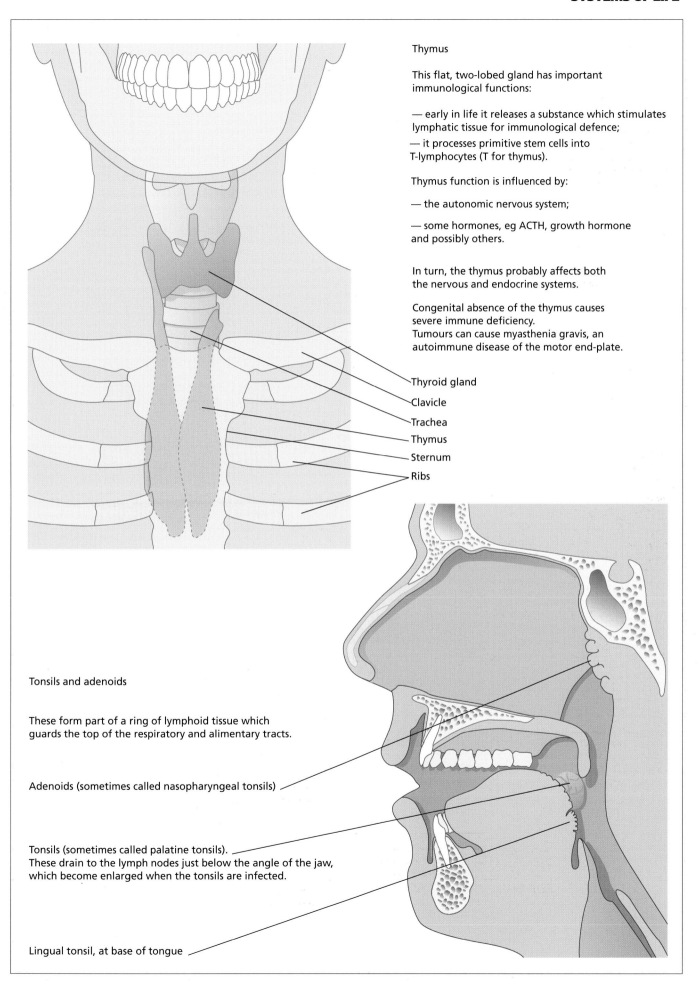

Thymus

This flat, two-lobed gland has important immunological functions:

— early in life it releases a substance which stimulates lymphatic tissue for immunological defence;
— it processes primitive stem cells into T-lymphocytes (T for thymus).

Thymus function is influenced by:

— the autonomic nervous system;

— some hormones, eg ACTH, growth hormone and possibly others.

In turn, the thymus probably affects both the nervous and endocrine systems.

Congenital absence of the thymus causes severe immune deficiency.
Tumours can cause myasthenia gravis, an autoimmune disease of the motor end-plate.

Thyroid gland
Clavicle
Trachea
Thymus
Sternum
Ribs

Tonsils and adenoids

These form part of a ring of lymphoid tissue which guards the top of the respiratory and alimentary tracts.

Adenoids (sometimes called nasopharyngeal tonsils)

Tonsils (sometimes called palatine tonsils).
These drain to the lymph nodes just below the angle of the jaw, which become enlarged when the tonsils are infected.

Lingual tonsil, at base of tongue

Spleen

This dark-purple, bean-shaped organ lies high up on the left side of the abdomen behind the stomach and against the diaphragm.

The functions of the spleen are to:

— destroy old red blood cells;

— form a reservoir of blood, which can be squeezed out into the circulation when needed;

— help release blood cells from bone marrow;

— help fight infection; people whose spleens have been removed or are not working properly are at risk of overwhelming infection, especially if they are also taking immunosuppressive therapy for malignant diseases.
Patients should be told about these risks and given immunisation and prophylactic antibiotics when appropriate.

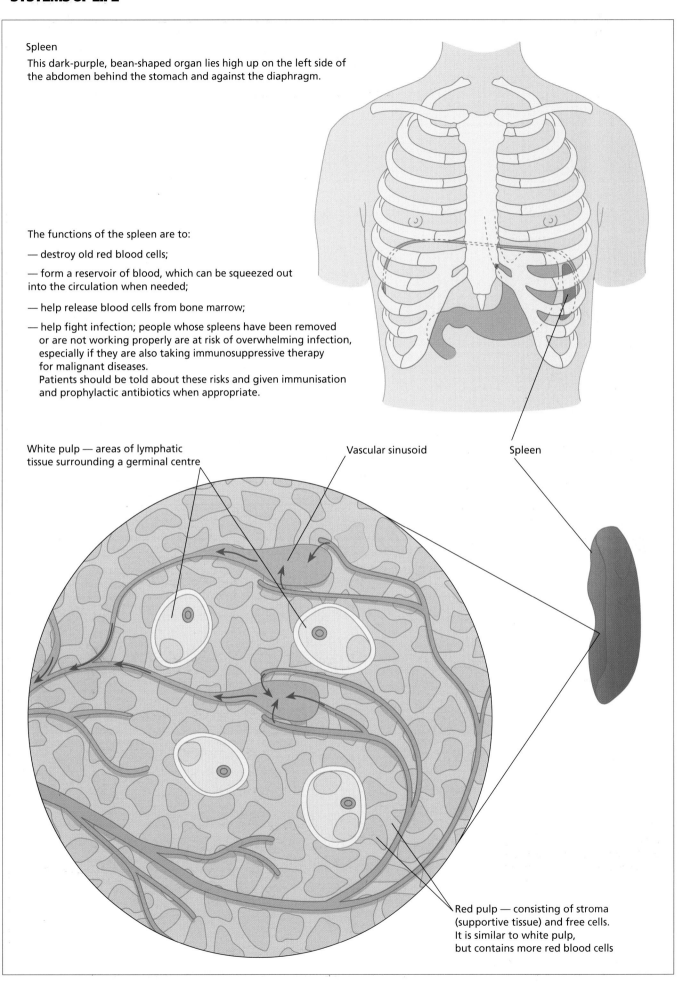

White pulp — areas of lymphatic tissue surrounding a germinal centre

Vascular sinusoid

Spleen

Red pulp — consisting of stroma (supportive tissue) and free cells. It is similar to white pulp, but contains more red blood cells

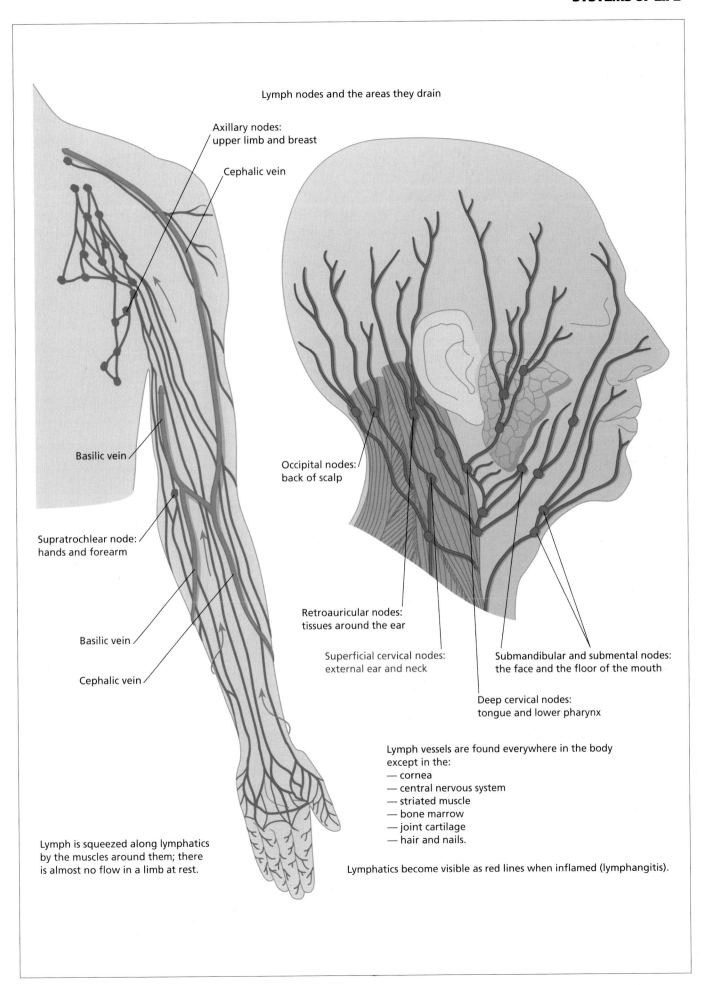

Lymph nodes and the areas they drain

Axillary nodes:
upper limb and breast

Cephalic vein

Basilic vein

Supratrochlear node:
hands and forearm

Basilic vein

Cephalic vein

Occipital nodes:
back of scalp

Retroauricular nodes:
tissues around the ear

Superficial cervical nodes:
external ear and neck

Submandibular and submental nodes:
the face and the floor of the mouth

Deep cervical nodes:
tongue and lower pharynx

Lymph vessels are found everywhere in the body
except in the:
— cornea
— central nervous system
— striated muscle
— bone marrow
— joint cartilage
— hair and nails.

Lymph is squeezed along lymphatics
by the muscles around them; there
is almost no flow in a limb at rest.

Lymphatics become visible as red lines when inflamed (lymphangitis).

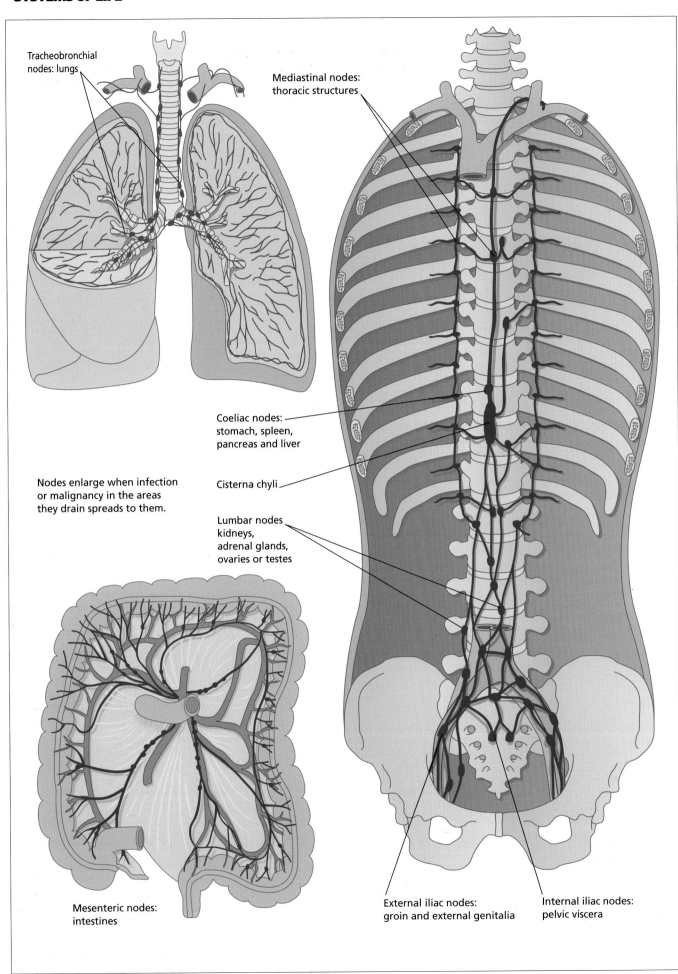

Tracheobronchial
nodes: lungs

Mediastinal nodes:
thoracic structures

Coeliac nodes:
stomach, spleen,
pancreas and liver

Cisterna chyli

Nodes enlarge when infection
or malignancy in the areas
they drain spreads to them.

Lumbar nodes
kidneys,
adrenal glands,
ovaries or testes

Mesenteric nodes:
intestines

External iliac nodes:
groin and external genitalia

Internal iliac nodes:
pelvic viscera

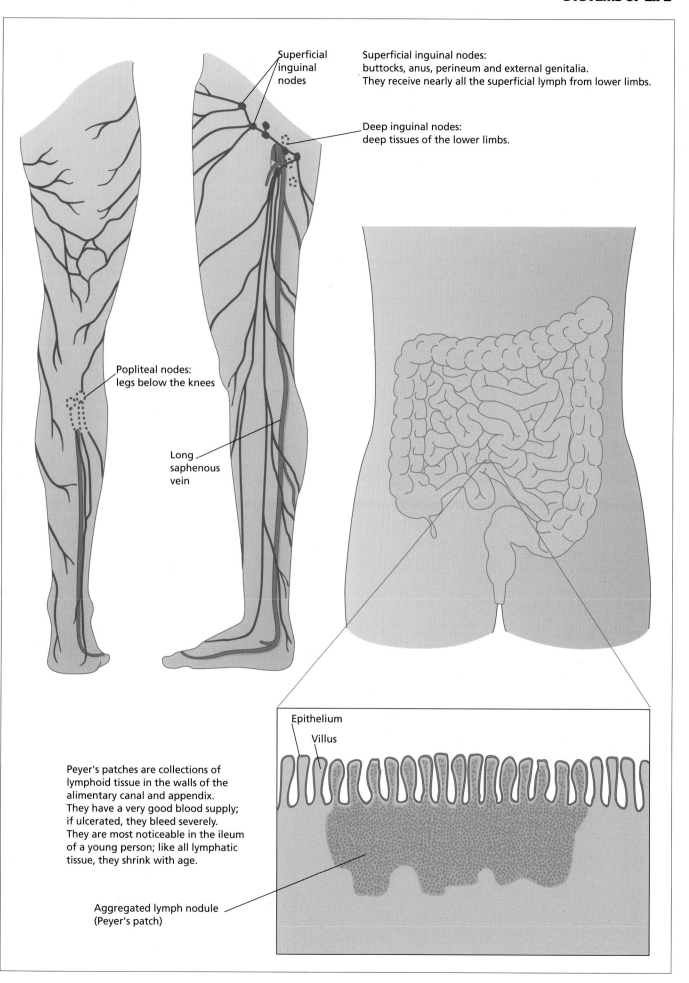

Superficial
inguinal
nodes

Superficial inguinal nodes:
buttocks, anus, perineum and external genitalia.
They receive nearly all the superficial lymph from lower limbs.

Deep inguinal nodes:
deep tissues of the lower limbs.

Popliteal nodes:
legs below the knees

Long
saphenous
vein

Peyer's patches are collections of
lymphoid tissue in the walls of the
alimentary canal and appendix.
They have a very good blood supply;
if ulcerated, they bleed severely.
They are most noticeable in the ileum
of a young person; like all lymphatic
tissue, they shrink with age.

Aggregated lymph nodule
(Peyer's patch)

Epithelium

Villus